DESCENDANTS OF MEDUSA

A Collection of Poems, Prose, and Essays

Nymeria Publishing, LLC

Nymeria Publishing LLC

First published in the United States of America by Nymeria Publishing LLC, 2022

Copyright © 2022 by Nymeria Publishing

All rights reserved. Except as permitted under the U.S. Copyright Act of 1976, no part of this publication may be reproduced, distributed, or transmitted in any form or by any

means, or stored in a database or retrieval system, without the prior written permission of the publisher.

Nymeria Publishing

PO Box 350747

Jacksonville, Fl 32235

Visit our website at www.nymeriapublishing.com

Print ISBN 9798985157277

Ebook ISBN 9798985157284

1st Edition

Printed in U.S.A

For the witches, they could not burn...
*Let's turn **them** to stone.*

CONTENTS

Rachael Lord- Damn the Thieves	1
Tinamarie Cox- Moored	3
Eleanor Ambler- Cycles	5
Shockie G.- Beautiful	7
T. Walters- Becoming Fury	9
Madisyn Schofield- She Was The Sun	13
Maggie Kaprielian- How to Console Your Grieving Younger Sister	15
S. N. Benenhaley- A Game	17
Rachael Lord- On the Axis of Grief and Gravity	19
Maegen McAuliffe O'Leary- The Damn Birds Are at It Again	21
Cat Webling- Beautiful Me	23
G.T. Sims- An Attempt to Put Words to Lesbian Love	25
Adrija Jana- and in Silence	27
Eleanor Ambler- Atmospheric Gender Dynamics	29
Allison Fradkin- Boob Ease	31
K. L. Champitto- Taste of Modesty	33
Rachael Lord- Born of Witches and Queens	35
Abbi Peters- Labyrinth	37
Elise LeSage- Siberian Woman, 5 C.E	39
Allison Fradkin- Holy Inappropriate	41
Morgan Bridges- 6/24/2022	43
A.F. Kaye- MISCARRIED	45
Maegen McAuliffe O'Leary- Spontaneous Abortion	47
Amethyst Bernard- to the little girl who hated pink	49
Shockie G.- Women Don't Burp	51
Lenora Brown- Maturity	53

Belinda A. Edwards- Stone Carrier	55
Amethyst Bernard- Yellow	65
Sarah Butkovic- Bacchus's Bar & Tap	67
Eleanor Ambler- Ballet Class on the Last Monday of November	69
Adrija Jana- On Femininity	71
Sophie Kuhn- Crimson Tinted Eyelids	73
Allison Fradkin- Soar Spot	75
Shelley Sanders-Gregg- No Heartbeat	79
S. N. Benenhaley- Herricane	81
G.T. Sims- Desert Hearts(break)	83
Deirdre Garr Johns- Untitled	85
Meet the Authors	87

Damn the Thieves

To the girl who dreamed
of being a princess—
your handmade crown
was always enough.

To the young woman who believed
in fairytale endings,
but thought love
meant the same
as starving herself—
eat the bread,
lose the boy who told you that.

To the daughter who fought
demons in her bedroom,
under the blanket of night, all while
wielding a broken sword—
you are stronger
than every villain in your head.

I see her sometimes
when my own eyes catch the mirror
damn the thieves, I think,
for taking your strength from you.

But in the next breath,
I whisper into the darkness:
look how you stole it back.

- Rachael Lord

Moored

She was told
she should reach for the stars
and then,
she was handed an anchor.

-Tinamarie Cox

Cycles

Sometimes I think I am healed of heartbreak.
I rise thrumming with the rhythms

of lifetimes, blood circling the stories
my mothers lived, breath expanding songs

through generations. I sing a round with the echoes
of their voices; I dance natural into my own.

When memory bleeds back, I lie hysterical, arteries
stretched and scattered about the earth. History says

I cannot be whole. My womb wanders homeless,
breaking the membranes that keep my brain

in sane states. Insane states tell me I am a home.
I am whole when I house a fetal man

in fatal agony. On days I cannot rise
I almost believe them. Let pain fill this aching

gap between my thighs; let something stop the flow
of traumas passed through rivers of red.

I sing my soul into one cloth;
I wrap your children in its freeing folds

                    -Eleanor Ambler

Beautiful

From birth, they will convince you that skinny is equivalent to beautiful...
to successful...
to happily married...
while looking different is a death wish.
Imagine being told your shadow takes up too much space in a world full of darkness
and your body with all its depth could never hold love.
They will tell you no one will ever love you until you love yourself.
But when you feed them confidence,
they will claim you are shoving unhealthy down their throat that you should be ashamed.
These bodies should not be on display.
I guess the scalpel be a forgiving deity, carving miracles into skin.
My body bleeding a prayer of hope.
Not ready for Nirvana but begging for a resurrection
like surgery be the new hara-kiri leaving me a person a new.
Like weight is the only thing holding a woman down as if gravity don't exist.
Peel off my layers say the scars will fade.
Why must we always have to sacrifice ourselves in order to be saved?

-Shockie G

becoming fury

the rape changed both of us
i may not be cursed by athena
or have hair that hisses
but i felt the need to
protect myself
to claim those
serpents as my own

every man was a threat
and we treated them in kind
you turned men to stone,
i, to objects,
something to play
with to forget
all of their harm
both statues
still, cold, and lifeless
no longer human for loving but
creatures hoping to harm us

we were both changed by
clever men
as you slept, he snuck in,
using trick mirrors to
defeat you
to even see you
a coward's power is his tricks
isn't it?

your head on the ground,
they called him hero

and i will not speak his name

when you were slain, i cried
for the fault was not yours
yet the mythology books call you
cruel, hateful, seeking vengeance
i say seeking justice

our rage exists as a just one
a source of power that
wells up within us,
bursting out at those
who wish to betray us
to feel our power--
rather, take it for themselves--
to keep us
doe-eyed and docile,
silent and submissive,
civil and complacent

Fear us

not monster, no, but
mortal--humanity too
seen by devilish eyes
defying them by
daring to survive

i see you -- hero

your strength
a sight to never be seen

will you grant me your gaze

cursing the men who look upon
me with malice and hate
to forever remain in their fear
as they behold the
beautiful monstrosity that
they turned me into
regretting ever stealing a glance

i see you
vibrant and alive
with flowers in your hair,
which hisses in delight
you--protector
of wretched women
symbol of painful resilience

here i kneel at your feet,
cleansing you of your
so-called sins
as i lay you down for
your eternal sleep
i will close your eyes
adorn you with hazel
and declare you, Medusa, human

you will rest, blessed,
knowing how many you saved
from the same fate that cursed you

i see myself in you--
guardian of wicked women,
trying to shield your children
from the harms of man

the rape may have changed us
but we do not break
instead, we turn our enemies
to stone and
protect our humanity
with hazel in our hair

                        -T. Walters

She Was The Sun

When she was away, he longed for her
To banish his dark and lonely nights

But when she returned, shining her brightest glory,
He ran for the shadows to lessen the strength of her shine

She was the sun who radiated her fiery love,
But he was the man unable to bask in her light

-Madisyn Schofield

How to Console Your Grieving Younger Sister

i. Get out of bed when you hear her sobs at midnight.

The walls separating your bedrooms are thinner than the list of your unshared memories. Your eyes are only half-adjusted to the darkness, and her screams are equally thunderous as they are devastating. As tempting as it is to bury your ears between the white linen sheets, realize that compromising your sleep isn't such a compromise when it comes down to the agony of your sister.

ii. Ask her what's wrong, but don't get defensive when she won't tell you why.

You and her talk incessantly. Survival seems unpromised on days where you don't communicate til you've hit the extremity of silence. But sometimes, shared silence can be just as soothing as an: are you okay? Sometimes, talking is overbearing when your own mouth mistakes explanations for screams. She doesn't owe you words, even after the fifth time asking. Remember that your presence is the fondest gift when compared to absence. So sit with her in this silence. Don't make her listen to it alone.

iii. When she finally tells you the reason for her weeping, prioritize the clouded eyes right in front of you.

When you hear his name, you'll long for nothing more than to wreak havoc on the life who's responsible for your sister's suffering. Save the unadulterated pettiness for the morning. In this moment, all of your attention should be directed to her. Do not tell her that she's wasting her time over a boy she won't remember in five years. You've told her that before, and although it's entirely true, she doesn't need to hear it again. Let her feel the fury of Ancient Greek goddesses, stripped of their own salvation. Let the wrath of Aphrodite speak volumes in your sister's bedroom.

iv. Do not leave her bedroom until she falls asleep. But when she asks for space, go down to the kitchen and pour her a glass of water.

She's not the same freckle cheeked, baby toothed sister she once was. She doesn't need her hand held but she still needs to know someone cares enough to reach out their open palm. She can make decisions, so let her make decisions. Listen. Absorb her words. Give her water but let her form a vast ocean.

v. Realize you've been here before.

You and your sister aren't too different. You've had nights parallel to these; full of looming thoughts as the world grows too quiet. You've boarded doomed ships before, unaware of the colossal storms preparing to flounder your strength. The only difference is, she has you. So see yourself in your sister. Sit with yourself from years prior:

Get out of bed for her.
Don't get defensive.
Prioritize her emotions.
Do not leave her bedroom.
Pour her a glass of water.
Share the silence that was
always too loud for her.

-Maggie Kaprielian

A Game

"It's just a game," he said.
My innocent eyes looked up at him.
I loved games, games of any kind.
"Just don't tell anyone about this."
My head nods eagerly,
Not knowing the contract I just signed.

It was such a long and tedious game we played,
One that became unwanted, unrecognizable, and unmemorable,
Until it wasn't anymore and it was the one thing that haunted my mind,
And kept me up late at night because I felt like it was my fault.

I don't know if I will ever be able to recover from being a victim of the game.

-S. N. Benenhaley

On the Axis of Grief and Gravity

I have learned
that the world does not stop
for your trauma,
it does not pause
for your grief.

No matter how hard you beg
or scream
or cry
or plead with every god
to rid his fingerprints
from your skin.

The world does not stutter, too,
when you cannot find the thoughts
to put your experience into words.

Your tongue ties tighter
each time they ask you
to tell
your story.

The world does not,
will not,
let you jump off
and come back when you're ready—
the world will make you believe such a thing
has made you stronger

but we all know that's a damn lie.

Instead,

you see,
this world
will spin you blind
and knock you sideways
but it keeps on going
and so will you.

-hold on, I've heard it gets better-

-Rachael Lord

The Damn Birds Are at It Again

These days everything seems to be
a message from the other side.
Surely, this is how women lose ourselves.
Open the door and start letting in
any old voice for a chat.

Surely, this is what gets us burned—
staying still too long,
listening too ferociously,
baring teeth without a smile.

                        -Maegen McAuliffe O'Leary

Beautiful Me

I am beautiful
    Me
    In my rolls and my pudge
    With the hard-earned grudge
    Against diets and fads
    That invaded my youth
    And took a beautiful girl
    Through a dangerous world
    And hurled beauty at her
    Like a weapon
    Poor thing

I am beautiful
    Me
    Whether you like it or not
    And how sad that the rot
    Of feeling then I was dead
    Tired of being me
    Made me feel I was wrong
    Just for being
    Without seeing
    The girl in the mirror
    She learned to fear her
    Reflection
    Poor thing

I am beautiful
    Me
    And it took me too long
    To realize my own song
    Was a symphony
    If I trust in me

I can be
Just as beautiful
As I dreamed I'd be
When I was that girl
Now I am a girl
A woman
That's beautiful

        -Cat Webling

An Attempt to Put Words to Lesbian Love

Strap wings to my arms with words of "yes and..."
Lift me up to the places between two people I never knew existed
To breath in feelings that my nostrils don't have names for
What is beauty if what creates it is fearful to some?
What is love if it is shared between two women?
When I think of beauty I think of the blue-grey tendrils that stretch across your widened eyeballs when you're lost in thought
When I think of love I think of the long, lithe limbs that pull me up from despair, lead me to unknown, and spin me around to twang-filled melodies
We are
You and I are
Smiles, applause, tears, and stares say, love
Stares, yells, laws, and gods say abomination

But when I look at you I know it is
It is
It is
Look at me
It is what we know is sure as your hand in mine in a universe of unsure
It is what I know has saved my life before it ending
It is what I know in every shred of my being that you couldn't even believe you've touched
And when the sun sets in the dream house of your embrace
And days turn nights turn years turn to the depths of eons
I lay my heart out next to yours
And listen to them thump together

-G.T. Sims

and in Silence

The sickly sweet smell of excess male perfume
The strong rotten smell of drunken breath
Assault her senses
A brutal assault
He comes closer

Suffering from the cramps of her monthly cycle
Tired from the hard labour of the household
She shakes her head no
It goes unnoticed
He comes closer

and unravelling
She starts chanting "No, no, no" like a mantra
Deaf ears are oblivious
The back of her knees hit the bed
He comes closer.

She screams "No!"
But the hand is strong, too strong
The scream is muffled, the tears are free
But water can't soak a rock
A few bangles break
The shards jabbing into her heart, twisting
Rivulets of blood flow out
More bangles break
Bangles tight and loose
He comes closer.

screams no more
It's eerily silent

She's no more with him
She's lying on her father's lap
She's playing with her little brother
She's reading his very first love letter-
"I'll never let any pain touch you..."
He comes closer.

The thread breaks
Was it weak?
Who knows? Maybe, beaten down
And worn out through the years
Now it is no more.

-Adrija Jana

Atmospheric Gender Dynamics

When I look up
at the clouds, I see the faces of men.
Puffy white cumulous, puff-chested
white man. Wisplike cirrus, wispy-haired
old man. They talk
loudly, 'I'm swell,' they say,
hop in their windcars and speed
through the sky, blocking the sun.
'We'll get those quotas met,' they say,
measuring the reach of their shadows.
They touch and watch themselves
fill.

When rain falls
it has shape, and substance. Clearly
outlined spermdrops boast their bombardment
of Earth. Drop down,
dust scatters. Phallic storms leave
flower petals ripped from their homes, lying
trampled in the darkness. Cloudbursts impregnate.
Crops spring up through factory floors, grow
in the maw of machines with metal teeth.
They are processed as profit before they learn freedom.
Manclouds say, 'look at that round bottom
line.'

When mist tiptoes in
I wonder who they are. Invisible everyone
silent rising they are there, gentle water, welcome
caress the clouds never see. They unfold
quiet across the land. 'May I offer

you myself,' they whisper, and they are
multitudes, infinitely more
than a single song of self. They feed the grass
with the soft shhh of she, the persistent thrum
of them, the living zing of ze. They are all
around, holding Earth, elevating
ever, freeform being in boundless
atmosphere

-Eleanor Ambler

Boob Ease

We'll always be buddies, bosom.
Partners in lime,
snooty pink,
cutie peach.
As long as you don't bust my tops
(which you would
if you could
but you can't
so you won't).

Of course, in my Maidenformative years,
they didn't exactly rack up points with me.
If mammary serves me correctly,
they were not my cup of teeny.
Convinced there was no better girl
than a sweater girl,
I was shelf-conscious,
a tit mouse,
a chest nut.

But somewhere along the bustline
I stopped being a boob
and realized that the breast things
come in small packages.
So there's no use crying over
frilled milkshakes,
even if they and the mounds
of whipped cream
are ties in size.

Because I don't need a push-up
to put me over the top.

I just need a good head on my shoulders,
not bra straps.
Once I headlightened up,
I was able to bounce back,
not up and down.
And now that I've stopped giving a hoot
about my humble hooters,
it's no Wonderbra that
I am 34A-OK.

-Allison Fradkin

Taste of Modesty

The word modesty tastes like poison in the back of my throat
It burns just as badly as the word whore
But when the word first touched my tongue at age 7 it tasted like bubblegum
Like the reward for acting the way I was supposed to

But whore
Whore tasted like a stranger's spit in my mouth
Like they forced their tongue on top of mine
Like it didn't belong in my vocabulary
Or anyone's

When I hear other people throw the word around
I wonder if they taste the poison too
Or if the problem lies in the fact that
Poison only tastes like poison
After it's already been swallowed

Modesty and whore seem like polar opposites
But to me, they are the same
Just different takes on putting women in their place
I am told to dress modestly
But am a whore regardless, if a man decides to lay a hand on me

Modesty may come in a colorful wrapper
But it's only handed out to women
It's the reward we didn't ask for
In a game
We don't want to be playing

But I've been playing this game since the moment I was
born with a vagina instead of a penis

So no
I will no longer swallow the poison
Or spit it out at other women
Because I know all too well
How an internalized patriarchy
Can destroy you
From within

-K. L. Champitto

Born of Witches and Queens

I am not the serpent
nor the stone
I wield not fire in my blood
but the rage of those who came before me
and with a smile on my cheeks, I will be
unafraid to look you in the eyes
and siphon your power
like I was put on this Earth
to do

we are the ones you should fear.

-Rachael Lord

Labyrinth

Look over your shoulder.
Don't make eye contact.
No, make *some* eye contact.
None would make me rude.

Flash a smile.
Make them feel comfortable.
I don't want to be labeled
as the girl with an attitude.

Don't speak your mind.
Bite your tongue.
Keep your comments minimal
or else you're a bitch.

"Where's your makeup?"
"Oh my gosh you look tired!"
"Dress modestly so you don't
end up in a ditch."

I need to lose weight.
I'm getting crow's feet.
My stretch marks are bad.
I need a drink.

My stomach isn't flat.
I should be more confident
but society tells me
how I should think.

My mind is a labyrinth.
A never ending maze of

of anxiety, guilt and
self doubt.

Each turn seems wrong.
I'm lost,
head spinning.
Let me out!

                    -Abbi Peters

Siberian Woman, 5 C.E.

Some would call it luck,
the way frost bloomed over my body,
sealing each skin cell in place.

My eyes fell out and I lost
    one ear,
        a fingertip,

but otherwise I'm still here,
lit up like a prize in my display case.

One dawn long ago, they found me in a cave
    along with: two clays pots
    a wooden ring,
    a copper coin,
    four coral beads.

And for days, I basked
in the glow of their machines, listening,
listening as they posed inquiries,
each answer pried from my stomach, ribs, and lungs.
How far did I travel?
What did I eat?
How well was I loved?

And now, and here,
crowds pay to see
me strung up and raised from the dead.

Toes, curled as if in pleasure;
    teeth, brown and bared.

If I'd a choice,
I wouldn't have liked to grimace forever, but
I try to bless each pointed finger,
each photo flash, each gape,

each child's whimper, hushed.
Is that a real dead girl? They ask.
And, in some other life, I flush. Some
would call it luck.

-Elise LeSage

Holy Inappropriate

Good morning, young ladies, and welcome to the first annual Pure and Simple Conference! I'm Mary Jo Genesis, and I'll be leading today's first breakout session, The Birds and the Believers.So many disciples at my disposal. Not even Mr. Christ's crucifixion attracted a crowd this colossal. I see each of you is wearing her virgini-tee as required, with its promotion of celibacy as desired. Seeing the words Cel Me More, Cel Me More printed across each chaste chest, I've got chills—they're purifying, and I'm oozing control. Self-control.

Ignorantly blissful and blissfully indoctrinated, and content with your mission in life: submission, you can't wait to create a family—nay, an army—for God. But you will wait. Not only that; you will throw your wait around. During the waiting period, you may find yourselves thrust into lust. These feelings you're experiencing are not unlike personal goals and higher education: they must be passionately denied. This is where self-control comes in. Along with self-something else.

According to Proverbs 31:13, a virtuous woman worketh willingly with her hands. That verse calls us to use faith-friendly fibers in the construction of our modest attire. Taking the characteristics of a virtuous woman out of context—taking anything in the Good Book out of context—is something we do religiously, so it's all hunky-dory.

If you are willing to work with your hands, as Jesus commands, waiting can be tolerable, pleasurable. Preferable. That's because a baby is not a female's only bundle of joy. She also has one generously applied to the exterior of her reproductive organs. It is called Clitoris. Repeat after me: Cli-tor-is. This, not creation, is our creator's most perfect design. Like you girls, Clitoris has a servant's heart: each and every one of its nerves serves the sole purpose of enabling you to experience the rapture righteously and regularly, thank God. (Thank you, God!) Those unsaved unbelievers don't call us Biblical Cliteralists for nothing.

Inside your swag bag is a rudimentary replica of Clitoris in the form of a pom-pom ball. Let's expedite its excavation, for upon location, you will embark on your very first pilgrimage to exultation. Where there's lubrication, there's liberation! Well? What are you waiting for? If Jesus can turn water into wine, we can turn ignorance into bliss. Because the gospel truth, girls, is that the Second Coming belongs to Christ, but the first coming belongs to you!

                    -Allison Fradkin

6/24/2022

I've imagined you more times than I can count.

May sound naive of me to dream of a child when the world is on fire, but I sketch drafts of you in the furthest reaches of my mind, tucked away where you'll be safe.

Far from the iron grip of politics.
Far from the relentless debate of a divided world.

Far from me.

I haven't met your father yet, but your eyes are the most magnificent shade of green — a perfect recollection of new spring growth. They'll disappear behind the apples of your cheeks, and you'll hate how it makes you look in pictures. Your hair will fall in your eyes in strands reminiscent of honey or wheat or late morning light. Your skin radiates the same internal glow you've always carried, casting a shadow on the Sun itself.

I reach out for your hands, much smaller than my own, and this image of you begins to falter. It trembles and flickers, and I struggle to find my breath — I shudder and blink back tears. The endless headlines read 'Roe v. Wade Overturned'. Countless times I cracked jokes of how you'd probably be a boy, a perfect antithesis to my sister's two girls. What if I'm wrong?

Oftentimes, I wonder if you were ever meant to be more than a dream.

My body exists in a state of imbalance, a teetering scale of hormones — nearly tripling my likelihood of a miscarriage. A miscarriage that could be brought to trial in some states.

Don't they understand how much I want you?

-Morgan Bridges

MISCARRIED

I wear your names like
    dog tags
    wrapped around my heart—
    casualties of a war
    you didn't sign up for.

                      -A.F. Kaye

Spontaneous Abortion

My husband is angry.
Men are always angry
about the wrong things.

He cannot see the light growing
through the crack where darkness bloomed
a mushroom cloud, dank
with mossy possibilities.

He cannot see the wishes made whole
by wishing for more of the same
despite the danger.

~~~~~~~~~~~~~~~~~~~~~~~~~-Maegen McAuliffe O'Leary

to the little girl who hated pink

you are not a girl anymore so
there's that.
you still hate pink but
you don't hate yourself
at least not as much.

you moved out
of the home that hurt you.
you quit your job
disappointed your parents
and yourself
at least for a few weeks.

you finally got the courage
to leave her for good.
although
she really didn't give you
a choice but
at least you recognize yourself now.

mom got better
dad got worse
it was so hard
not to turn into them
but you buried the bad
under the shaky foundation
only for it to come up
lavender.

                      -Amethyst Bernard

Women Don't Burp

Women Don't Burp He says.
They should learn to
Swallow it down
Hold it all in
Let it fester in the pit of the stomach.
This is how we stay strong eating ourselves alive from the inside.
Swallowing air to keep our cool until it builds up
Says I cannot hide anymore
And the anger crawls out our throats escaped gasses and unkind words.
Try not to say something you can't take back
lays across the room like a rotten burp.
They say its unladylike to act this way.
There is no excuse.
Women are supposed to hold it together
hold it down and never spill over
until she is alone out of any man's sight
only then is she allowed to free herself and her belly of all the days sours.

-Shockie G.

Maturity

Noun

the state, fact, or period of being mature.

honestly? it's just a lot of blood.
loose teeth and scraped knees and
your first time staining clean sheets.

and I guess
it's sort of pretty-
like how a forest fire burns
neon hot
against a bruised sky
sort of compelling
in that fatalistic sense,
like you can't look away.

I ordered "captivating",
I asked the waiter for "alluring" and "unmissable" and
in the way all that blood was beautiful,
I guess "spectacle" is close enough

-Lenora Brown

Stone Carrier
Turning life into stone

I was a daughter. As a daughter, it was the place of silence where I fell into a barren landscape, hiding, and avoiding the sharp stares of a mother, who turned me to stone. Like Medusa, a look into my mother's face, one frown, and I became deaf and dumb, falling back into step, eyes lowered, following her back into Hell.

Who was Medusa? A Gorgon, a beautiful maiden that was raped by Poseidon in Athena's temple. Athena, enraged by this transgression, did not punish the powerful God, but attacked the defenseless maiden, turning her into stone, a powerful fierce monster. It was Poseidon who took advantage of the young one, but it was Athena in her wrath that turned Medusa, the beauty, into the hideous. I recently saw an image of Medusa, scaly, snakes undulating like seaweed for hair, dark circles around her eyes, and a tear, clear and fresh as a raindrop in the corner of eye. Is this the image of Medusa when she realized that she was not going to be saved by Poseidon? Is this when her disbelief froze and turned to rage? I imagine Medusa moving through a dark cool cave, listening for footsteps, waiting for her father, or maybe Poseidon, to save her. How long did she wait? When did she give up hope? When did the frozen tear thaw and give way to rage? When did Medusa finally embrace her fierceness by turning life into stone?

I wonder who my mother's Athena was, who turned her from an innocent girl, the youngest of eight, into the strong woman, who survived by her will, turning others into stone. What were her challenges, her movements, her transformations that had her stand as the fierce one with the weapon of criticism, of the stare, that turned me, her daughter, into a cool, immobile stone. Who witnessed my mother's sadness, her fierceness, her brokenness, as her frozen emotions thawed. I wonder if my mother was pushed into silence. If her young voice was stifled by living in East Texas, in a rural community, with seven siblings, four brothers and three sisters, with the sign of slavery attached to their names, O'Connor, and the sign of the slave master's pleasure visible in my grandfather's features, a mulatto. The O'Connor boys were handsome and all in the community knew Monroe's boys. Some of the girls were less fortunate--One, light, good hair, but married to an abusive husband, bore five children. She died young, in silence, only the cancer spoke of the misery in her life, devouring cells, devouring her.

Medusa, the stone maker, reminds me of my Aunt Cat. She, blue black, was the darkest girl of four and the darkest child of eight. She was the oldest girl; I imagine her life in the 1920's. Sister to three older brothers, living on a farm working from sunrise to sunset, undervalued and maybe under loved. She escaped and went to school in Boston. My Uncle, her older brother, a train porter reached out a hand bringing her north to Boston, to live another life. She met her Poseidon, a man of power, virile, and married. She became pregnant and returned home, birthing a baby boy, blue black, continuing the tradition of outcast. My Aunt, like Medusa, was angry. We, the children, learned to skirt around her, never lingering too long. I learned this the hard way. I was young, younger than six, because I hadn't started school. She convinced me to let her cut my bangs. She cut them. As I looked in the mirror watching, a flash of rage fluttered across her face. She cut my bangs, almost to my scalp.

Hair in the black community has always been important and profitable. The first black millionaire was Madam Walker, who invented the hot comb in 1905. Then to make sure our kinky hair was even straighter; the chemical hair relaxer was discovered, also, in the early 20th century. Movie after movie has given witness to the importance of hair in the black community. The funniest, Chris Rock's 2009 documentary entitled Good Hair, focuses on the issue of how African American women have perceived their hair and historically styled it. Rock was inspired to make the movie after his three-year old daughter asked him, "Daddy, how come I don't have good hair?" She has curly, wiry hair typical of many people of African descent. She had already absorbed the perception that curly hair was not "good."

Children in my black community were often victimized, or ostracized, because of skin color or hair texture. I joined these ranks with unruly bangs too short to press, too nappy to blend in with other pressed hair, too weird to be fashionable. My bangs, little beads of nappy-ness, became a badge of betrayal, a badge of innocence lost. By cutting my bangs, my aunt showed a hostility toward me that was beyond my young age. Like Athena, she lashed out at the innocent, the young. Who was she attacking with this viciousness? Who was she defending herself against? In this act, I collected a stone from her. I never trusted or embraced her willingly again.

Even on her deathbed, her nieces, and nephews, five of us, told stories, each of us adding a stone to her memory, because each of us was given a memory stone of her rage and unhappiness to carry. Each story varied in severity, but each had an emotional impact. My light skinned cousin, wavy good hair, begins the story telling. He lived with her for months during her cancer treatment. During this time, she refused to feed him and of course did not pay him. He begins stealing her canned goods and eating them while she sleeps, but she always knew. She knew what was taken and began to lock her food cabinet. Who had starved her, who had withheld nourishment from her? What memories haunted her so that even in the end she was unable to relinquish her stones?

After my aunt drove my cousin away, she was alone struggling with cancer, my husband at the time and I went to see her, driving two hours from Santa Barbara to Riverside, CA to visit. During our short visit, she worked us like donkeys in the summer heat from the moment we arrived until the moment we left. She worked us so hard and was so demanding that we did not visit her again.

Around her death bed as we were telling stories about our interactions with her, we learned that Stanley, her son, her only child, our cousin, had tried to physically hold us, his female cousins, by force. He had waited for us to be alone and had tried to kiss or to grope us. Another stone was gathered because we told no one until now. Who knew that Poseidon was among us. Was Athena, the one who sided with him, also present? Who turned a blind eye to this? What within us kept us from telling? Who allowed this Poseidon to be in our midst, training for the future?

At her funeral, we sat as her neighbor sang her praises. We could not believe that someone admired her, someone respected her, that someone called her a friend. We looked at each other, convinced that this woman had wandered into the wrong funeral. Even in death, we blamed her for her stony heart and for the stones she carried in her life; she was

"dark" in a world that embraced light. She was like Medusa-
- misunderstood and betrayed. After our stories, we gathered our grievances, and placed them in her coffin, closing the lid in darkness while our stones continued to echo her stories, echo her sadness, and echo her rage. I did not see the tear in the corner of her eye, for she had long turned into stone. Did my aunt teach my mother to stare to control? Did she turn my mother's young innocence to stone? Who were the stone bearers in her family? Was it her mother, Josephine, my grandmother? Or was it her grandmother, Emma, my great grandmother? In 1927, when my mother was born, could one afford not to be a stone bearer? Could one afford to have wild black children roaming in the South?

Only in silence the word.

Once I was walking at the Abo Pueblo just south of Albuquerque, New Mexico. This pueblo had been abandoned since 1673. A combination of disease, drought, famine, and Apache raiding led to the abandonment of Abo. There is a large red stone church that rose from this barren landscape. It was November, the sky was clear, the weather warm, and no one was there. As I walked this site, I wondered if I should bring back a stone for my personal medicine bundle. I wondered if any stone would want to leave this sacred place and if it was selfish to carry an ancient stone from home. As I was leaving, I remembered the old saying that stones are incredible storytellers. One odd, shaped stone stared back at me. I bent down and at that moment I became a conscious stone carrier.

This stone is teaching me to witness, to be a carrier of ancestral wisdom stories, without judgement. I realized it is important to not judge the stories- because then we have the tendency to "whitewash" them to distort our history. As this blood red stone is carried from its ancestral land, I remember memories of childhood. The sound of horse hoofs on a paved road, while we children rode in the wagon with Monroe my grandfather, while Black Gal, his only horse, pulled the wagon, going to the store for a soda. Memories of Old Black Gal roaming free the entire year, and in the summer, us chasing her through fields with the bridle in order that we could ride her, floats through my mind's eye. I also have fond memories of playing in the front yard making mud pies and of frost falling on collard greens, and peanuts dug up from their summer slumber. This red stone silently witnesses my life, and I silently witness the lives of the stone carriers before me in my family.

I see them, my ancestors, lines of women, blue black extending back through time, forming a chain, even those lost at sea, join hands from their watery resting place, extending the chain from shore to shore, all the way back to our tribal home. Here the women carry baskets on their heads and babies on their backs. These women flow like water from one activity to another. From this line of women, we, their American ancestors, we, those taken, those fortunate enough to survive the voyage, became stone bearers. Those, who sunk down into their knowing, to survive the New World. Those who turned stony eyes on their babies, willing them to be silent, turning them into stone. Then becoming invisible as other children were sold off to new plantations, as other young girls were noticed by their plantation-owning fathers, as other sons were carried off to sire a strong breed of field hands. In silence was their protection. In stone, wisdom. Turning oneself or others into stone in this situation was a protective power. It froze innocence, it froze life.

Again, I reflect on Poseidon, the God who raped Medusa, and his brothers, Zeus, and Hades. Each ruined lives of the innocent, the young, the vulnerable, seducing them in the temples, dragging them into the underworld, into dark places. Yet to survive when we go to the dark place, we must come back singing. As the O'Connor girls became stone carriers, they attempted to save their children, reminding us to not talk about the activities in the house when we were outside of the house. This rule emerges from the portal of slavery, each slave child was warned to not discuss slave quarter business, when they were at the big house. We became stone carriers, carriers of secrets, carriers of stories, carriers of burdens handled to us throughout time.

I recently suffered a betrayal. I was enraged, fully embodying Medusa in her fury. When I analyzed the situation and the level of rage I possessed, it was out of balance; it was reflecting all the stones I have collected and have been carrying over the years. How does one relate to fury without turning others into stone? I no longer believe in turning the other cheek, but I also do not believe in an eye-for-an-eye. How does one contain the fury? How does one speak without one's fury turning another into stone? How does one break the chain?

Perceval cut off the head of Medusa, and from her blood flowing into the sea, red coral was formed. A friend of mine made me a pair of earrings, coral hung with white and grey pearls and a lava rock bead. Beautiful earrings that I wear, as a reminder that Medusa was a victim of betrayal. A victim of a woman who needed revenge but could not fight the power structure. Instead, she fixed her cold eyes on that which was young, loving, alive, and turned her into stone. Turned her into one who would not be able to love, one who would never be able to nurture, and one who would only bear witness through her stony glare. Only in this darkness, the light, only in this theatre generation after generation of stone bearers, turning their daughters into stone, because they were turned into stone themselves. Did they reach back to the root, looking for their Poseidon, the powerful man that shifts shaped beauty into an object that was then destroyed. How does one track the culprit, if we do not see?

I am stone, holding the memory of water.

It was April, a time straddled between spring and summer in the high desert. I am in Dixon New Mexico right after it rained, puddles of water still held at the surface before it seeped into the desert sand. I am here meeting with my teacher, and she is holding the lineage of the Peruvian bone throwers. Today, we walked in the arroyo following a little ribbon of water, which is flowing back into the Rio Grande.

I walk up stream, like salmon, to a place unknown. Each step is a movement away from the familiar, each step, into a place of wildness, each step thoughts drop away, as water moves and clears my thoughts. As I walk, I am stone, solid deep memories of twists and turns of the broken places and fractured dreams, witnessing movement, remembering. I am also water, flowing into the river, washing away traces of guilt, washing away memories. Out of water we crawled to shore dragging seaweed behind us on flappers that transverse the universe. Water holds my birth, water holds memory. I am a river stone, holding the embrace of water betwixt and between the worlds of things.

I realize that Medusa's rage was cooled by water. And from this something beautiful was created. In combining the element of stone and water, the hard and the soft, the tear at the corner of my eye softens hardened memories of ancient wrongs. Now I whisper our ancestral stories on the wind, I call my ancestors to come and sit by the fire. I will not let their memories like Medusa's be distorted. My stories remember the innocence lost, and the shape shifting of what was left of it, into hard, unmovable, witnesses, stone carriers. I embrace my ancestors, light a candle, and acknowledge them, and their efforts to keep us safe. On my altar, I will also burn a candle for Medusa. I am her kin. I understand, I embrace her. And in the warmth of our embrace, stone carrier to stone carrier, we live.

-Belinda A. Edwards

yellow

The untamed flames in my mind disappear
The moment her skin touches mine.
Illuminating the dark parts of my heart,
She knows exactly where I keep the matches.

I think of her and all I see is
Yellow.
She is warmth and her burden is
Light.

I want to swim in her eyes
And dance with her energy.
I have never felt so at home
Until she held me in her arms

                        -Amethyst Bernard

Bacchus's Bar & Tap

I spot a man made from Venus across the bar.
he sifts through the musty crowd of mortals
stalking with feline elegance.
a debonair set of eyes like fishbowls of blue,
they cut through the dust on the dancefloor.

he weaves through the throng of heartbeats
the stark lighting like a dagger to his jaw.
he's an angel of porcelain with ivory skin,
an ethereal face handcrafted with care.
the goddess of beauty has sculpted a masterpiece.

A woman from Flora sits next to me at midnight.
the goddess of flowers, a bloom of green love.
cloaked in vines from the Isles of Paradise
and laced with a saccharine scent of the earth.
i gaze with rapt silence, stunned into submission.

she shows me how to grow my own garden that night.
saffron chrysanthemums sprouting to life
and rose petals red for the very first time.
i've been surrounded by flowers for years
yet never learned what a lotus tastes like.

-Sarah Butkovic

Ballet Class on the Last Monday of November

he said he could see
our thanksgiving dinners hanging
out of our stomachs,
as though our fullness was shameful.
if there is a problem with thanksgiving
dinner shouldn't it be the
heavy history of genocide and not
the weight of a teen girl's thighs?
our bellies growled the dissent our mouths
could not voice. our bodies tried
to take space even as we shrunk
into our shy, hungry souls.
sixteen shouldn't mean skipped meals and
dizzy bus rides. sixteen should be
sweet, maybe a little
sticky, like the caramel dripping off
an apple, bitter juices running rivulets
across a sugary surface.
apples bloat, he told us,
and should be avoided for their
roundness. where was our snake, voice
of reason saying, eat,
my lovelies. you are beautiful
when you are full?

-Eleanor Ambler

On Femininity

If I wear my Father's shirt, do I become a boy?
If I cut my hair short, do I cease to be Feminine?

What is Femininity anyway?
Must Femininity stand with downcast eyes and cover her head?
Must Femininity lower her voice and sit just so?

Must Femininity sweat in the kitchen and cater to Man's every whim?
Must Femininity close her eyes, and cast aside every dream?

If that is what Femininity is to you,
Then I'm sorry to say
I'm not Feminine

Must Femininity not protest for her rights and freedom?
Must Femininity not vote in a democracy?

And yes, I'm a girl
But I don't need to prove that
By wearing clothes you choose
By sitting the way you want me to
By wearing my hair the way you ask
If I wear my father's shirts, you say
People might start to think I'm gay

So what if they do?

I know myself
And for me, that's enough.

I don't need your validation, nor your advice
I choose to exercise my freedom of choice, my Right

And I don't need to be Feminine for love
And I will not change myself
For those who truly love me
Will accept me for who I am.

-Adrija Jana

Crimson tinted eyelids
Liquid black teardrops dripping
Down

                        And down

                                              And down

Reflecting in pools on her cheeks

Her skin is angry and her soul is on fire
Ferocious and fierce
But only

                        When she is alone

                                              In her room

                      -Sophie Kuhn

Soar Spot

You know something?
I got sand.
That's why I came to the beach.
I heard they were running low. Heh.
Speaking of hearing things,
I wish I had some tunes.
That tribute to transformation, "I Am Changing,"
would really hit the spot right now.
Well, not the sore spot.

But I don't mind listening to the sound of my own voice.
I never really noticed it before, but it's...present.
Pleasant. Much more mellifluous
than something off of your Greatest Hits album,
which includes such scintillating singles as
"Diss You Much,"
"Proud Marry in Haste, Repent at Leisure,"
and the pièce de no résistance,
"You Can't Stop the Beatdown."

Except I can. I did.
I stopped the beatdown.
You knew my motto:
Batterer up, three strikes I'm out.
You'll never have the pleasure of seeing me cry anymore.
Or the pain of seeing me smile.
In fact, you won't see me any kind of way, ever again.

See, you thought our song went:
I'm tellin' you from the start
I can't be torn apart from my guy.
But see, that is unapologetically uninspiring.

So on my album, the song goes
I'm tellin' you from the start
I can't be torn apart by my guy.

I know the first time leaving is the hardest—
first is the worst and all that—
but once you go black-and-blue,
you—I—never go back.
So you might think that this is one of those
"If at first you don't succeed,
try, try again" initiatives,
that they call it escapism because
it's nothing but a fantasy.
But I know something you don't:
I can take the y off "emergency"
and put an e there instead,
and then I've earned
a resurgence of emergence.

Words to live by.
Which is why I'm going to beat the odds
my first time out.
Well, maybe not beat 'em,
but "overcome" just sounds so
underwhelming.
I got guts for days.
Weeks, months, and beyond.

I can't take all the credit for my courage though.
Got to give gratitude to Sofia
—from The Color Purple, not The Golden Girls.
Her song "Hell No," about refusing to be cruising
for a bruising,
is what got me to make tracks in the first place.

A person hears something often enough,
she starts to believe it.
She starts to repeat it. Out loud.
I'd croon, you'd cringe—and criticize:
"I know why the caged bird sings.
She's a Maya Ange-loser.
Come on now, don't pout.
You know I'm only teasing,
and still I get a rise out of you."

And what did I ever get out of you?
Nothing but another bouquet of your
sorry-not-sorry-ass flowers,
the kind perfect for playing
that time-honored game of
"He Shoves Me, He Shoves Me Not."
That's right—I'm playing games without you,
and guess what?
I can identify 'em.
None of that baseless accusation B.S.
What games was I ever playing with you, huh?
Trouble?
Aggravation?
Pac-Man?

Well, since you neglected to specify,
I picked my own game to play:
Pack-Your-Bags-and-Leave-That-Man,
where every woman's a winner.
Now that's something to sing about:
He's got no power
No power no more
Over me.
Formerly sung by The Exciters,

presently sung by The Exiters.
When did I get so
infuriatingly inspirational?

Must be when I realized that
I am the wind beneath my
uncaged wings, that
underneath the coat of war paint
I applied to the bruises
was a brave face
just waiting to be put on.

Someday, even when those bruises
are gone but not forgotten,
they'll still be souvenirs of survival,
and they'll still be a sore spot.

But now that I'm no longer under
your skin, your thumb, or your spell,
I can spell that word a little differently:
s-o-a-r.

Hell yes.

-Allison Fradkin

No Heartbeat

It started as tiny spots of blood.
"No big deal" I thought...
But then there was more...
I called my husband.
We called the doctor.
Then my mind starting whirring with the unthinkable,

                unimaginable,

                              unbearable...

"No, it can't be..." I told myself as I drove to the hospital.
Lying on the table I couldn't stop shaking...
trembling lips,

                hands,

                        every inch of me, it seemed.

Then the sudden c o l d on my belly felt like ice in an already too-cold room. I squeezed my husband's hands in nervous anticipation... a mix of fear, trepidation, and nausea swept over me. I silently prayed as the Doppler swept my belly for any signs of... life.
Then the words came...
those dreaded words that I never wanted to hear...

            "I'm sorry but there's no heartbeat."

                  No heartbeat.

My baby had no heartbeat.

And, in that moment, I felt as if I had lost mine.

                -Shelley Sanders-Gregg

Herricane

Herricane.
Slowly, but forcingly coming towards you.
Her willowing waltz turns into a sensual salsa,
But before you know it the harsh waters are surging.
Wind is uprooting the foundational roots of 100-year-old
trees before your eyes. The flood waters rise and wash out
cemented expectations and rigid stereotypes.
She is a force to be reckoned with,
A wrecking ball through sexism and misogyny,
A breath of fresh air and feminism.
No. A gasp of greatness,
That fills your lungs because you have been deprived so
long that it almost hurts to take in any more.

-S. N. Benenhaley

Desert Hearts(break)

Her heart dropped into her gut
and out of it.
Splatting onto the dust-covered sidewalk
as the summer sun
baked it warm.
The stagnant air rose perfumed from flowers they had
picked
caught in her lungs.
Her empty body crumpled, dry and broken
grass next to the neighbor's house rough against her cheek,
like their sleeping cat.

And just like that:
love was dead in the desert.

-G.T. Sims

Two days ago, the grass was an even spread of green.

Then. Heavy rains and supple land.

Now. The mushrooms—
white brown black—demand permanence
over the earth,
ripe and swollen.

The mushroom population propels itself
upright, uprooting the unassuming stalks of grass.

And what of the grass strangled and left
to rebirth itself after its own death?

How can it withstand this shadowed living?
It is hard enough to find the light
without being looked down upon.

-Deirdre Garr Johns

MEET THE AUTHORS

Rachael Lord is a writer, activist, and professional actress from Fort Myers, Florida, where she lives with her husband and three rescue dogs. She is the author of Fragile Hearts Club (Nymeria Publishing, 2021). When not writing, Rachael enjoys reading romance novels, playing Stardew Valley, and dismantling the patriarchy. http://www.rachaellord.com

Tinamarie Cox lives in Northern Arizona where she writes to escape her mind and explore the universe. Her poetry has been published in *Nevermore Journal*, *The Elevation Review*, *Oddball Magazine*, *The Sirens Call*, and others. You can follow her on Instagram@tinamariethinkstoomuch and Twitter@tinamarie_cox

~

Eleanor Ambler (she/her) is the author of *Ballet is my Boyfriend*, a chapbook from Bottlecap Press. Her poetry has

been featured in *The Foundationalist, LUX Creative Review,* and as part of a musical score for the Rhode Island Women's Choreography Project. In addition to her work as an author, Eleanor is a professional ballet dancer.

Shockie G is a Black, Lesbian, Spoken word Poet. Currently the 2022 Grand Slam Champion in Pittsburgh PA, she has won multiple Slamcompetitions both online and in person. You can find samples of her work within Read or Green's "Out Loud" LGBTQ Anthology and a previous self-published chapbook "Shattered Emotions Scattered Thoughts" Currently working on a manuscript for a full collection, you can catch her in and out of Open Mics, Workshops and other spaces that allow for connection with our communities.

Maggie Kaprielian is a poet from Maryland. She is an Editor-in-Chief for the Erehwon Literary Arts Magazine and a poetry editor for The Moco Review. Her work has been featured Letters to Lovers Zine, Soultalk Magazine and Lit. 202.

Madisyon Schofield's love for creative writing formed at a young age when she started writing fanfiction on the platform Wattpad; after several years, she began writing original short stories and poems. "She Was The Sun" is her first poem to be published.

∼

T. Walters is a poet, writer, and musician living amongst the orange trees. Whether they're jamming on the guitar, cuddling up with their dog and a library book, baking bread or pulling needle through thread, Tea is presently enjoying life as a rebel without a clue.

∼

S.N. Benenhaley is the previously published author of *Saturn and Their Rings*. In their time outside of writing, they are a clinical mental health counselor that works in a private practice. The topic of mental health heavily influences their writing style and advocacy, taking their life experiences with mental illness and trauma as the forefront of their work.

∼

Maegen McAuliffe O'Leary is a poet and mother from the Pacific Northwest. Her poems have been featured in publications from Querencia Press and Quail Belle Magazine, and her debut chapbook, Bodies to Bury the Hunger, is available from Bottlecap Press. Her selected poems are also available on Instagram @m.f.mca.

Cat Webling is an actress and author based in Kansas. Scifi, fantasy, and poetry are her main stays when she's not writing about literature, theater, gaming, or fan culture. She is an active member of the Kansas Authors Club, and daylights as a copywriter for hire. Cat writes from her home, which she shares with her loving partner, adorable son, and several very cute cats.

K. L. Champitto (They/Them) is a writer of Poetry, Children's Literature, plays, and YA contemporary novels. When they aren't working, they enjoy spending time with their two children and 2 rescue Pitbulls. You can find them on Instagram @authorchampitto.

Adrija Jana is a passionately creative writer based in India. She mostly creates poetry pieces based on her personal experiences as well as social issues she is passionate about. Her work mostly revolves around protest against period poverty, marital rape, and advocating for freedom of choice, apart from emotional self-lived experiences. She is inspired by writers such as Margaret Mitchell and Nayyirah Waheed, as well as the minutiae of everyday life. She believes that creative pieces that let the innate imperfection shine through truly touch hearts.

Allison Fradkin (she/her) delights in applying her Women's & Gender Studies education to the creation of satirically scintillating poems, prose, and plays that (sur)pass the Bechdel Test and enlist their characters in a caricature of the idiocies and intricacies of insidious isms. An enthusiast of inclusivity and accessibility, Fradkin freelances for her hometown of Chicago as Literary Manager of Violet Surprise Theatre, curating new works by queer playwrights; and as Dramatist for Special Gifts Theatre, adapting scripts for actors of all abilities. Allison's auxiliary activities include vintage shopping, volunteering, and tending to her thespian tendencies.

Abbi Peters is a 27 year old mom of a wonderful baby girl. She started writing about 6 years ago as an outlet and hasn't stopped since. She mostly writes poetry but is currently working on a young adult fiction novel.

~

Elise LeSage studied English at Virginia Commonwealth University, where they received the undergrad award for poetry (2018) and creative non-fiction (2019). They have served as an editor at Amendment Literary and Arts Journal, Wind-Up Mice, and Plain China Anthology.

~

Morgan Bridges is currently a senior in the English Department at Georgia Southern University, Statesboro. Before transferring to Georgia Southern University, Morgan obtained her Associate's in Fine Arts for Music from Abraham Baldwin Agricultural College in May 2019. Aside from her literature studies, she works as Managing Editor with the George-

Anne Media Group and enjoys writing both poetry and creative nonfiction.

A.F. KAYE is a poet and published author for her works in both poetry and memoir essays. She obtained her Bachelor's degree in English with a specialty in comic scripting and creative writing from Virginia Commonwealth University. Her mother wanted her to be a doctor, but you can see how well that turned out.

Amethyst Bernard (they/them) is a queer, non-binary poet and artist from Long Beach, California. An upholder of the healing power of poetry, Amethyst's work focuses on themes of queer love, gender and identity, and mental health. Their poem "Calluses" won second place in Nymeria Publishing's poetry contest in March of 2022, and they are currently creating free, virtual poetry workshops for queer writers.

Belinda Edwards is an African American writer. She is from "the red earth of East Texas, where the peanuts grow dreaming of winter harvest; and blacksmiths, farmers, teachers, and janitors with strong backs and quick wit toil." She was recently nominated for the 2023 Pushcart Prize and had a piece published in the Santa Fe Literary Review 2021 Fall issue. She earned her M.A. degree in Counseling Psychology from the University of California, Santa Barbara and currently lives in Santa Fe, NM.

Sarah Butkovic received her BA in English from Dominican University last May and recently received her MA in English from Loyola University Chicago. As a writer, she has published creative and journalistic work within and outside an academic setting,  including a news piece in a local Chicago paper. Ray Bradbury is her most frequent literary muse as well as her favorite author.

 **Sophie Kuhn** is a Canadian poet currently studying Social Work in Thunder Bay, Ontario where she lives with her partner and cat (Connor and Gideon, respectively). She began writing poetry two years ago and is inspired by the work of Ursula Le Guin, Al Purdy, and E.E Cummings. Growing up, she wanted to be a librarian and author, and has a passion for theatre, literature and social justice. Inspired by Marxism, feminism and philosophy she explores topics of self love, being Queer, empowerment, trauma and nature in her writing.

Shelley Sanders-Gregg is a writer and poet from St. Louis, Missouri. She is a wife and mother of four children. She holds a Master's degree in social work and much of her poetry centers around hope and healing, nature, and the joys of motherhood. You can find more of her work on IG: @sgreggwrites

Lenora Brown is currently a student at university studying to be a Paralegal. She lives in Maryland with her mom and geriatric pug, Dena.

G.T. Sims is a queer, multifaceted artist based in Salt Lake City, Utah. As a sound sculptor, DJ, spoken/written poet, drag performer, and storyteller for the past 6 years, they have a passion for exploring the ways in which art exists and is expressed&received sonically in the endless soundscapes in this world and beyond. They are honored to be a part of this publication as this is the first time their written work has been published.

Deirdre Garr Johns resides in South Carolina with her family. Nature is an inspiration, and poetry is a first love. Much of her work is inspired by memories of people and places. Her poetry and non-fiction have appeared in several publications, which can be accessed through her website www.a-museofonesown.com.

www.ingramcontent.com/pod-product-compliance
Lightning Source LLC
LaVergne TN
LVHW041618070526
838199LV00052B/3197